AF484727

PROPERTY WEALTH

A Legacy Built Through Real Estate Empowerment

BY
SCOTT L GORDON

Copyright © 2024 by Scott L Gordon

All rights reserved. No part of this publication may be reproduced, distributed, or transmitted in any form or by any -means, including photocopying, recording, or other electronic or mechanical methods, without the prior written permission of the publisher, except in the case of brief quotations embodied in critical reviews and certain other non-commercial uses permitted by copyright law.
*Library of Congress Control Number: **2024926041***

Published by Book Writing Genie
Cover design by Book Writing Genie
ISBN: Printed in the United States

TABLE OF CONTENTS

Dedication

This book is dedicated to my beloved family—my children, Brandon and Taylor, and my grandchildren—who are the heart of our legacy. May this work serve as a testament to perseverance, faith, and the importance of family.

Acknowledgment

First and foremost, I give thanks to God, who is the head of my life. To my wife, Kristi, thank you for your love, inspiration, and support as we embarked together on this journey to build wealth. A special thanks to Frances Reed, Purina Williams, and Rue Ramsey for your invaluable assistance in proofreading and offering thoughtful insights that enriched this work. To Katie and Andrew McGoy, thank you for helping me manage my time effectively and ensuring that I could complete this project with focus and dedication and my friend who was my first realtor and has been there since day one Carol Pankey- Davis.

To my church family, Calvary Baptist Church in Sapulpa, Oklahoma, thank you for being a source of strength, community, and faith. This book is a tribute to all of you who have walked with me, inspired me, and lifted me in prayer. May God's blessings continue to be upon us all.

Finally, A heartfelt thank you to one of my greatest business partners, Melvin Matthews, and his wife, Carol, whose mentorship has guided me along the way.

About the Author

Scott L. Gordon

Scott L. Gordon—a name synonymous with faith, community impact, and real estate empowerment—brings his lifelong passion and experience to the pages of *Property Wealth: A Legacy Built Through Real Estate Empowerment.* Hailing from Sapulpa, Oklahoma, Scott's journey is a testament to his deep-rooted commitment to ministry, community development, and generational wealth building.

A graduate of Sand Springs Public Schools, Scott furthered his education at Tulsa Vo-Tech and Oklahoma Junior College and earned a diploma from Rhema Correspondence Bible School. His educational foundation culminated in an associate degree in Biblical Studies from the Oklahoma School of Religion Langston, a Bachelor's in Pastoral Ministries, and a Master's in Christian Education. This extensive training has anchored him as a spiritual and community leader, driven by a calling to empower others.

Scott's journey with his wife, Kristi (Rider/Blalock) Gordon, and their two children, Brandon and Taylor, is a story of faith and family. After being licensed and ordained by the late Reverend Ervin Ruth, Scott embarked on his ministry path, initially serving as a youth minister before becoming the Senior Pastor of Calvary Baptist Church in Sapulpa in 2002. Under his leadership, Calvary Baptist has transformed into a "hospital" for the soul, offering spiritual, mental, financial, and physical support for all who enter.

Scott's heart for service has taken him across the globe, providing faith and aid in Nicaragua, Ghana, Nairobi, Kenya, the Dominican Republic, and London. His work as a Hospice chaplain for over two decades, along with his commitment to prison ministry, school outreach, and nursing home devotionals, reflects his dedication to touching lives in profound ways.

Beyond his ministry, Scott is a cornerstone of community development. He has led initiatives through the W.L. Hutcherson YMCA, One Church One Child, the Hope Community Center, and the Creek County Literacy Program. His leadership extends to roles within the Sapulpa Ministerial Alliance and Tulsa Christian Together, as well as on the boards of the Terence Crutcher Foundation, Manna Mission in Ghana, and the International Fellowship of Christian Businessmen. During his tenure with Camp Loughridge from 1998 to 2005, Scott helped steer strategic planning, capital campaigns, and major building projects that continue to benefit countless families.

Scott's entrepreneurial journey is equally inspiring. As CEO of SLG Properties LLC and co-founder of 180 Realty LLC, Scott has built a multimillion-dollar real estate business centered on revitalizing low-income neighborhoods, creating homeownership opportunities, and fostering financial independence. His expertise in real estate is not only evident in his portfolio but also in his commitment to teaching others. Scott's passion for empowering people to create generational wealth through real estate shines in

Property Wealth, where he shares invaluable insights and practical strategies for achieving financial freedom.

An active member of the National Baptist State Convention Inc. USA, Southern Baptist, and Full Gospel Baptist, Scott also holds a "Pastor's Alternative Teaching Certificate." As President of Scott L. Gordon Ministries, he has authored two impactful books, leads weekly broadcasts on CTN, and continues to uplift his community with his faith-driven leadership.

Scott's vibrant approach to life, leadership, and ministry is unmatched. With a spirit-filled commitment to seeing lives transformed, Scott L. Gordon brings readers not only a guide to wealth but a call to action to embrace purpose, faith, and legacy-building. Through *Property Wealth*, Scott offers more than words—he provides a pathway to a life of impact, success, and meaningful change.

Introduction

Property Wealth – *A Legacy Built Through Real Estate Empowerment By Scott L. Gordon* is both a practical guide and a deeply personal account of Scott Gordon's transformation into a successful real estate investor. This book provides readers with a structured approach to navigating the complex world of real estate investing, blending hands-on advice with the real-world experiences that shaped Scott's path to financial independence.

Scott's journey began with a clear motivation: to find a sustainable way to build wealth and achieve financial security. Dissatisfied with the volatility of traditional investments and the uncertainties of conventional business, he turned to real estate—an asset he found uniquely resilient, stable, and promising for long-term growth. He discovered that rental properties, with their consistent income potential and appreciable value, could offer the predictability and control he sought. This realization became the cornerstone of a carefully developed strategy that, over years of disciplined execution, grew into a multimillion-dollar portfolio.

In this book, Scott systematically unpacks every phase of his investment strategy, designed for investors at various stages. For beginners, Scott's insights demystify the essentials of real estate, offering step-by-step guidance on building a profitable portfolio from the ground up.

For those already versed in the basics, the book dives into advanced techniques for maximizing cash flow, scaling investments, and mastering market dynamics. From setting financial goals and evaluating properties to navigating the nuances of property management and mastering tax strategies, Scott provides a comprehensive toolkit designed to help readers build lasting wealth.

However, this book goes beyond tactics and strategies. Scott offers an honest look into the challenges he faced and the critical lessons he learned along the way—lessons about resilience, adaptability, and the importance of thorough due diligence. He emphasizes that real estate investing is not without its setbacks and requires a disciplined, hands-on approach to overcome unexpected obstacles. Each chapter reflects Scott's commitment to providing readers with not only technical insights but also a realistic understanding of the commitment and persistence essential to success.

Throughout Property Wealth, Scott also highlights the importance of community and the role of relationships in real estate investing. Building strong networks, fostering trust with tenants, and ensuring properties are well-maintained are central to his philosophy. He views each investment not just as a financial transaction but as a service to the community, creating lasting value for both himself and those impacted by his properties.

For those determined to pursue financial freedom through real estate, Property Wealth is more than a guide—it's a roadmap grounded in experience and a professional manual for anyone committed to succeeding in the real estate market. Whether you're just beginning or are looking to scale an established portfolio, this book equips you with a proven framework, strategic insights, and the confidence needed to achieve meaningful, sustained success.

Chapter 1
Tangible Assets, Tangible Goals – My Real Estate Journey

The motivation behind my decision to invest in rental properties.

Property investments and how I established clear financial goals and devised a long-term plan to achieve them. Growing up, my perception of wealth was shaped by the stories of individuals who had made fortunes in the stock market or through successful businesses. Their tales were often filled with exhilarating highs and crushing lows, leaving a lingering sense of uncertainty. I longed for stability, a steady income stream that would weather economic storms and provide a cushion against financial hardships.

What I realized later was that these stories, as inspiring as they were, often lacked a crucial element—consistency. The stock market, while lucrative for some, was unpredictable, and starting a business came with its own set of risks, from changing market trends to operational hurdles.

It was during my later years that I stumbled upon the concept of rental properties and the numerous benefits they offered. The idea of owning a tangible asset class that generated consistent monthly income while simultaneously appreciating in value sparked an intense curiosity within me.

Rental properties seemed to offer a solution to that very uncertainty I had been trying to escape. With real estate, I wasn't simply speculating or relying on the success of a product or company. I was investing in something physical, something people would always need—a place to live. That tangibility gave me a sense of control I hadn't found in other wealth-building avenues.

After hours of research, exploring real estate markets, and analyzing potential returns, I became resolute in my decision to invest in rental properties.

But making the decision wasn't enough—I knew I had to establish clear financial goals. I wasn't just buying properties; I was designing a roadmap for the life I wanted. I broke down my goals into short-term and long-term milestones. Initially, I focused on acquiring my first property, ensuring that it would provide positive cash flow.

Once that was achieved, I expanded my focus to building a small portfolio—properties that could eventually generate enough income to replace my traditional salary. Each property was a step closer to financial independence.

I also had to refine my approach to financial planning. It wasn't just about saving enough for a down payment or covering the mortgage; it was about understanding the full scope of expenses— maintenance costs, property management fees, taxes, and potential vacancies. I wanted to be fully prepared. In doing so, I created a financial cushion that allowed me to handle any unexpected hurdles. This sense of preparedness gave me the confidence to keep going.

As I began to see my financial goals materialize, my plan evolved. What started as a way to build wealth turned into a passion for creating value—not just for myself but for the tenants whose lives would be improved through well-maintained homes. I began to view property management as not just an investment but as a service. This mindset shift allowed me to build relationships with tenants, creating a sense of community within my properties, which, in turn, resulted in longer-term tenants and stable income.

Over time, I also diversified my real estate investments. While residential properties provided a solid foundation, I eventually explored commercial real estate and short-term rentals.

Each step added another layer of security to my financial future and broadened my understanding of the market. What began as a desire for stability transformed into a comprehensive, long-term wealth strategy.

Setting financial goals and creating a long-term plan.

Setting clear financial goals was essential in framing my investment strategy. I embarked on a comprehensive evaluation of my financial situation, identifying my income, assets, liabilities, and expenses. By quantifying my current financial position, I was able to understand where I stood and set realistic targets for the future.

This initial step, though daunting, was critical. It forced me to face the raw numbers and gave me clarity about what I could realistically achieve.

I had to get honest with myself about my spending habits, uncovering areas where I could cut back and save more for investment opportunities. It was eye-opening to see the gap between where I was and where I wanted to be—but also incredibly motivating.

Next, I focused on establishing specific investment objectives. I delineated both short-term and long-term financial goals, creating a roadmap that would guide me toward financial independence. These goals included achieving a stable monthly cash flow, building a diversified real estate portfolio, and eventually generating enough passive income to cover all my living expenses.

In breaking down these goals, I realized that financial independence wouldn't happen overnight. I had to celebrate small wins, like securing my first property, ensuring it produced positive cash flow, and learning how to effectively manage tenants.

Each milestone gave me the confidence to set even bigger goals. It became less about just owning properties and more about fine-tuning a system that worked for me.

With my goals outlined, I turned my attention to crafting a long-term plan that would enable me to realize them. This involved meticulous research into various real estate markets, identifying potential locations with high rental demand and promising growth prospects.

I didn't just rely on surface-level information; I dove deep into demographic trends, future development plans, and job growth statistics for each area. I was looking for markets that would sustain their appeal over the years, not just temporary booms.

I also learned the value of networking and speaking with local real estate agents, property managers, and even other investors to get an insider's perspective on potential markets.

I educated myself on the intricacies of property financing, lease agreements, property management strategies, and the legal aspects of being a landlord. Understanding these components not only protected me legally but also equipped me with the tools to avoid costly mistakes that could derail my progress. For example, learning how to structure a solid lease agreement helped me avoid tenant disputes, and understanding property financing options enabled me to leverage my assets smartly without overextending myself.

Equipped with this knowledge, I carefully analyzed my risk tolerance and determined the optimal investment strategy. I decided to adopt a conservative approach by initially investing in properties that promised steady cash flows and had the potential for long-term appreciation.

This conservative strategy allowed me to build a strong foundation before taking on more ambitious projects. It wasn't about quick wins but about ensuring each investment was sustainable in the long run.

By taking a steady, calculated approach, I could minimize risks while maximizing growth potential. Over time, I began to diversify my investments—expanding into properties in different regions and varying property types to further protect against market fluctuations.

My plan also entailed creating a diversified portfolio, gaining exposure to different markets, and mitigating risks associated with economic downturns or fluctuations in specific regions.

Diversification was my hedge against unpredictability. If one market slowed down, another would likely still be profitable. By spreading my investments across different areas and types of properties—single-family homes, multi-family units, and even commercial real estate—I could balance out the risks.

This strategic diversification gave me the confidence to keep growing, knowing that my portfolio had built-in safeguards.

The decision to invest in rental properties has been spurred by a deep-rooted motivation for lasting financial freedom and security. But it wasn't just about financial freedom; it was about the lifestyle I envisioned—one where I wasn't tied to a desk or dependent on a paycheck.

Real estate allowed me to pursue that dream by creating passive income streams that would sustain me and my family for years to come.

By setting clear financial goals and creating a well-structured long-term plan, I was able to lay the foundation for a successful investment journey. Every decision I made was anchored in those goals. Even when the real estate market fluctuated, having that long-term vision kept me grounded.

My plan wasn't to get rich quickly; it was to build something sustainable that would outlast me. And now, with the right framework in place, I can say that I'm well on my way to achieving that.

In the subsequent chapters of this book, we delve into the practical aspects of investing in rental properties, highlighting my experiences lessons learned, and providing invaluable guidance to those aspiring to embark on a similar path.

I'll share the mistakes I made and the strategies that worked, with the hope that others can learn from my journey and chart their own course toward financial independence.

Chapter 2
Market Smarts for Real Estate Investors

---•●•---

In the ever-evolving landscape of real estate, it has become imperative for investors to build a solid foundation of knowledge and understanding before making any investment decisions.

In this chapter, we will dive deep into the important aspects of understanding the real estate market, conducting thorough market research, developing a comprehensive investment strategy, and finding the right location to identify lucrative investment opportunities.

Understanding the Real Estate Market

To start, it is crucial to grasp the dynamics and intricacies of the real estate market. Understanding market conditions, trends, and factors that drive supply and demand is essential for making informed investment choices.

The real estate market is like a living organism—constantly shifting based on both local and global factors. This makes it critical for investors to not only understand the present conditions but also anticipate future changes.

The real estate market is influenced by a myriad of factors, such as economic conditions, population growth, job markets, infrastructure developments, and interest rates.

For example, a booming job market can drive up demand for housing as more people move into an area, whereas rising interest rates might cool down demand by making mortgages less affordable.

Likewise, infrastructure improvements—such as new highways, schools, or business hubs—can drastically affect property values.

By staying abreast of these factors, investors can anticipate market fluctuations and make sound investment decisions. It's not enough to react to changes after they've already occurred; savvy investors stay ahead by predicting trends.

A deep understanding of economic indicators like GDP growth, unemployment rates, and inflation can provide insight into the future direction of the real estate market.

When you learn to recognize early warning signs—such as a slowdown in building permits or an increase in interest rates—you position yourself to adapt and capitalize on market opportunities.

Conducting Thorough Market Research

Thorough market research is the next step in building a solid foundation for your real estate journey.

PROPERTY WEALTH

Conducting extensive research involves gathering data on various real estate markets, understanding the demand and supply dynamics, and analyzing historical and current market trends.

In today's digital age, investors have access to vast amounts of data at their fingertips, making it easier than ever to evaluate market conditions. However, it's important to know which data matters most and how to interpret it.

For instance, simply looking at property prices won't give you the full picture—vacancy rates, rental yields, and future development plans are equally critical in determining the viability of an investment.

This research includes studying demographic information, rental rates, vacancy rates, average property prices, and future development plans.

Demographic shifts can provide essential insights into the future demand for real estate. Is the population of an area growing or shrinking? Are younger people moving in, or is the region aging? These trends can affect everything from rental prices to the types of properties that will be in demand in the coming years.

Collecting this data and interpreting it will help you identify opportunities and assess the profitability of potential investments. It's also important to think beyond the immediate data.

For example, understanding future development plans—such as the construction of new shopping centers or the extension of public transportation—can reveal emerging areas of growth.

Similarly, researching property tax trends, school districts, and crime rates will give you a holistic view of the market. A thorough approach ensures that you don't just chase current hot spots but invest in areas with sustained potential for long-term appreciation.

Developing a Comprehensive Investment Strategy

Once armed with a wealth of information, it is time to develop a comprehensive investment strategy. It's important to remember that real estate investing isn't a one-size-fits-all approach. What works for one investor may not work for another, so your strategy needs to be tailored to your financial goals, risk tolerance, and timeline.

Your strategy should consider key factors such as your budget, the type of properties you want to invest in (residential, commercial, multi-family), your preferred markets, and the amount of leverage you are comfortable using.

For instance, some investors prefer to focus on rental income, seeking properties that offer a steady cash flow, while others may prioritize long-term appreciation in value, even if it means foregoing higher immediate returns.

Additionally, your strategy should include contingency plans to account for market fluctuations or unforeseen expenses.

In real estate, unexpected events are the norm—whether it's a sudden economic downturn or an unexpected repair bill. Having an emergency fund or a flexible exit strategy can be the difference between surviving and thriving in a challenging market. It's essential to create a plan that is both ambitious and adaptable.

Finally, ensure your investment strategy evolves over time. As you gain experience and as market conditions change, your approach should be flexible enough to adapt. What worked for you when you purchased your first property might not be the best approach as you scale your portfolio or as new opportunities arise. By periodically reviewing and refining your strategy, you stay ahead of the curve and ensure long-term success.

Finding the Right Location

Perhaps one of the most important decisions you will make is finding the right location for your investments. In real estate, location isn't just a cliché—it's the cornerstone of a successful investment. A property's value and potential for return are deeply connected to its geographic setting, so choosing the right area requires careful consideration and research.

When looking for a location, it's important to evaluate both macro and micro-level factors. On a macro level, look at the overall economic health of a city or region. Is it a growing area with job opportunities? What is the population growth rate? Cities with strong economies, expanding industries, and population booms are prime candidates for real estate investment.

On a micro level, delve into specific neighborhoods. Even within thriving cities, not all neighborhoods are created equal.

Proximity to schools, public transportation, and amenities such as parks or shopping centers can make one area far more attractive to potential renters or buyers than another.

Look for areas with upward trends in property values, declining crime rates, and plans for future development. Emerging neighborhoods—those on the cusp of revitalization or development—can offer significant upside potential. Investing early in these areas can lead to substantial appreciation over time, especially if new infrastructure or businesses move in. However, it's also essential to balance this with an understanding of the risks involved in betting on an area's future growth.

By identifying locations that align with your investment strategy and offer the potential for long-term growth, you ensure that your investments have the highest possible chance of success. Remember, location is one factor you can't change once you've purchased a property, so it's worth taking the time to get it right.

Through a deep understanding of the real estate market, thorough market research, a well-thought-out investment strategy, and careful selection of location, you set yourself up for success in the ever-evolving real estate landscape. Each of these steps lays the groundwork for identifying lucrative opportunities and building a robust real estate portfolio that stands the test of time.

Identifying Investment Opportunities

Identifying investment opportunities is the culmination of understanding the market, conducting research, and selecting the right location. At this stage, everything you've learned comes together to guide your search for the perfect property. It's about being proactive, diligent, and sometimes even creative in finding deals that align with your investment strategy.

This involves actively seeking out properties that align with your investment strategy and match your financial goals. A crucial part of this process is knowing what type of property will work best for you. Are you looking for a single-family home in a suburban area that offers steady cash flow? Or perhaps a multi-unit property in an up-and-coming neighborhood that promises significant appreciation over time? Matching your financial goals—whether it's immediate cash flow, long-term equity growth, or both—with the type of investment is key.

Opportunities can be found through various channels such as listings, real estate agents, networking, or even off-market deals. While traditional channels like online listings and working with real estate agents are important, don't underestimate the power of networking. Attending local investor meetups, connecting with property managers, or even speaking with neighbors in areas you're interested in can sometimes lead to off-market deals or inside knowledge of upcoming opportunities. Off-market deals, in particular, can offer less competition and the potential for negotiating better terms.

By employing due diligence and thoroughly evaluating potential investment opportunities, you can identify properties that offer favorable cash flow, appreciation potential, and attractive returns on investment. Due diligence goes beyond just the numbers—it involves inspecting the property for structural issues, understanding the local rental market, and even researching the neighborhood's future growth potential.

For example, a property that seems like a great deal on paper may come with hidden costs like expensive repairs or vacancy issues. Or, a location with high current demand could stagnate if there are no future development plans or economic drivers in the area. Properly vetting each investment ensures that you're not just chasing surface-level returns but making a sound, long-term decision.

Building a solid foundation in real estate investing is a fundamental step toward achieving success. Each investment you make becomes a stepping stone, contributing to the overall growth of your portfolio. By remaining patient, disciplined, and informed, you'll be able to navigate the complexities of the real estate market with confidence, laying the groundwork for sustainable success.

Remember, successful investors don't just look for properties— they seek out opportunities that align with their strategy, adapt to changing markets, and continually refine their approach based on experience and insight.

Finding The Right Location & Identifying Investment Opportunities.

Understanding the real estate market, conducting thorough market research, developing a comprehensive investment strategy, and finding the right location and investment opportunities are crucial components of this foundation. By carefully considering these elements, you will position yourself for long-term profitability and wealth accumulation in the dynamic world of real estate investing.

Some websites that can help with finding properties or rental properties

- Zillow – https://www.zillow.com
- Realtor.com – https://www.realtor.com
- Trulia – https://www.trulia.com
- Apartments.com – https://www.apartments.com
- Craigslist – https://www.craigslist.org/

These websites offer a variety of search options and filters to help you find properties that meet your investment criteria. Additionally, they often provide information on rental prices in different areas, allowing you to compare options and make informed decisions. Beyond these, platforms like Redfin and Homes.com can also be valuable resources, offering unique insights and additional listing options that might not be available on the aforementioned sites.

One option for looking at real estate market prices is through Multiple Listing Services (MLS) available in your area. These platforms provide a comprehensive database of properties for sale, including price data, property details, and market trends.

Access to MLS data often requires working with a licensed real estate agent, but the depth and accuracy of the information available make it an indispensable tool for serious investors. MLS listings typically include detailed property histories, allowing you to track price changes and understand market movements over time.

Additionally, real estate websites such as Zillow, Redfin, and Realtor.com mentioned earlier, also provide market information about property prices, sales trends, and market forecasts. These platforms frequently update their data to reflect the latest market conditions, offering features like price estimates, neighborhood analytics, and predictive market trends. Utilizing these tools can help you stay ahead of the curve and make proactive investment decisions.

A Simple Breakdown of the Strategy for Making Informed Decisions in Real Estate Investing

1. Define Your Investment Goals and Criteria:

Determine Your Desired Return on Investment (ROI): Assess what kind of returns you are aiming for, whether it's short-term gains through flipping properties or long-term income through rentals.

Identify Your Risk Tolerance and Investment Timeline: Understand how much risk you are willing to take and over what period you plan to hold your investments.

Establish Criteria for Property Type, Location, and Budget: Decide whether you want to invest in single-family homes, multi-family units, commercial properties, or other types. Define the geographic areas you are interested in and set a clear budget to guide your search.

2. Conduct Thorough Market Research:

Analyze Market Trends and Property Prices in Your Target Area: Look into current and historical data to understand how property values have changed and where they are heading.

Look for Emerging Neighborhoods with Growth Potential: Identify areas that are on the rise, where infrastructure projects or new businesses are attracting residents and increasing demand.

Consider Factors Like Job Market, Population Growth, and Economic Indicators: A strong job market and population growth can drive demand for housing, while positive economic indicators suggest a healthy real estate market.

3. Develop a Comprehensive Investment Strategy:

Define Your Investment Strategy (e.g., Buy and Hold, Fix and Flip, Rental Properties)

Choose a strategy that aligns with your goals and expertise. Each strategy has its own set of challenges and rewards.

Set Financial Goals and Create a Budget for Acquisitions and Renovations

Plan your finances meticulously to ensure you have sufficient funds for purchasing properties and making necessary improvements.

Create a Timeline for Property Acquisition and Exit Strategy

Outline when you plan to buy properties and under what conditions you would sell them, ensuring you have a clear plan for each stage of your investment.

4. Find the Right Location and Identify Investment Opportunities:

Explore Different Neighborhoods and Property Types: Visit various areas to get a feel for the local market and identify which types of properties are in demand.

Attend Local Real Estate Events and Networking Opportunities: Engaging with the local real estate community can provide insider information and potential partnerships.

Work with Experienced Real Estate Agents and Professionals for Guidance: Leveraging the expertise of seasoned professionals can help you navigate complex transactions and uncover hidden opportunities.

5. Evaluate Potential Properties:

Conduct Due Diligence on Properties of Interest, Including Inspections and Property Analysis: Ensure that the properties you are interested in are structurally sound and free from significant issues that could affect their value or profitability.

Compare Property Prices, Rental Rates, and Potential Returns: Analyze the financial metrics of each property to determine its viability as an investment.

Consider Factors Like Property Condition, Location, and Rental Demand: A property's physical state, its location within the market, and the demand for rentals in the area are critical factors that influence its investment potential.

6. Make Informed Decisions and Execute Your Investment Strategy:

Analyze All Information Gathered to Make a Decision Based on Your Criteria: Use your research and analysis to choose properties that best fit your investment goals.

Negotiate Favorable Terms with Sellers and Secure Financing: Effective negotiation can lead to better purchase terms while securing the right financing options ensures your investment is financially sound.

Implement Your Investment Plan and Monitor Property Performance Regularly: Once you've acquired a property, actively manage it to ensure it performs according to your expectations, making adjustments as necessary to optimize returns.

By following this structured approach and utilizing the resources available, you can make informed decisions in real estate investing and increase your chances of success in the market. Moreover, staying adaptable and continuously educating yourself about market changes and new investment strategies will further enhance your ability to thrive in the competitive real estate landscape.

Building a solid foundation in real estate investing is a fundamental step toward achieving success. This foundation not only supports your initial investments but also provides the resilience needed to navigate the inevitable challenges and opportunities that arise in the dynamic world of real estate. By committing to ongoing learning and strategic planning, you set yourself up for sustained growth and financial prosperity.

Chapter 3
Financial Pathways – Strategies for Real Estate Investors

In the world of real estate investing, financing plays a crucial role in turning investment opportunities into tangible assets. To navigate this financial landscape effectively, it's essential to understand the various options available, build strong relationships with lenders, and develop strategies for maximizing cash flow and managing debt.

Exploring Financing Options: Mortgages and Hard Money Loans

One of the most common financing options for real estate investments is the mortgage. A mortgage allows investors to leverage their capital by securing a loan against a property. Mortgages typically offer longer terms, lower interest rates, and lower monthly payments compared to alternative financing options. However, it's crucial to understand the mortgage terms, including interest rates, repayment schedules, and any prepayment penalties, as these factors can significantly impact overall profitability.

Another financing option to consider is a hard money loan. These are short-term, high-interest loans secured by the property itself rather than the borrower's creditworthiness. Hard money loans are advantageous in situations where conventional financing is not available or when a speedy transaction is required, such as when bidding on distressed properties or flipping homes. However, investors should carefully weigh the pros and cons, as higher interest rates and fees can affect cash flow and long-term profitability.

For example, investors using hard money loans may need to exit the deal within 12 to 24 months to avoid significant financial strain. This means having a clear strategy for either selling the property or refinancing into a lower-interest loan.

Understanding the risks associated with this type of financing is essential, especially when markets fluctuate, as rapid downturns could leave investors unable to refinance or sell at a profit.

Expanded Options: Conventional, FHA, VA, USDA, and Portfolio Loans

When seeking financing for real estate investments, investors should also explore several other options available through banks or other lenders:

- **Conventional Loans:** These traditional mortgages offer competitive interest rates and terms, but they come with stricter eligibility requirements, making them ideal for investors with strong credit scores and stable incomes.

- **FHA Loans:** Backed by the Federal Housing Administration, FHA loans have lower down payment requirements and more flexible credit criteria. They're an attractive option for investors with limited funds or less-than-perfect credit histories, particularly for first-time buyers.

- **VA Loans:** Available to veterans, active-duty service members, and eligible military spouses, VA loans offer favorable terms, including no down payment and no private mortgage insurance (PMI) requirements. For investors with military backgrounds, these loans provide a unique opportunity to enter the real estate market with minimal upfront costs.

- **USDA Loans:** Designed for rural property investments, USDA loans offer low interest rates and require no down payment, making them ideal for investors looking to purchase properties in eligible rural areas.

- **Portfolio Loans:** Unlike conventional loans, portfolio loans are held by the lender on their balance sheet rather than being sold to investors. These loans offer more flexible terms and eligibility requirements, which can benefit investors with non-traditional financial situations or those seeking unique investment opportunities.

It's important for investors to recognize that portfolio lenders can often be more open to creative deal structures, such as cross-collateralization, which can allow an investor to use equity in multiple properties to secure new financing. This opens up new possibilities for larger and more complex real estate projects.

Each loan type has its own advantages and disadvantages, so investors should evaluate their financial situations, investment goals, and eligibility criteria when choosing the best option. Factors like interest rates, down payments, and repayment terms play a pivotal role in determining the right fit.

Building Relationships with Lenders: Key to Favorable Financing

Developing personal relationships with lenders is critical to securing favorable financing terms. Establishing trust with banks, credit unions, and private lenders who specialize in real estate investments can provide you with access to valuable insights regarding their requirements and preferences.

Lenders often look at factors like credit scores, down payments, and debt-to-income ratios when deciding whether to approve financing. By understanding these requirements, investors can position themselves as attractive borrowers. Networking with local lenders and maintaining regular communication can make a significant difference in the quality of financing you secure.

Expanding on Lender Requirements

Lenders are not just focused on your credit score—they also evaluate your overall financial health. Understanding what they are looking for allows you to improve your standing and get better terms. Here are a few additional factors lenders assess:

- **Loan-to-Value (LTV) Ratio:** The percentage of the loan compared to the value of the property. A lower LTV means lower risk for the lender.

- **Debt-to-Income (DTI) Ratio:** A measure of how much of your income is spent on debt repayments. Keeping this ratio low improves your chances of securing a loan.

- **Property Condition:** Lenders often look at the condition of the property. A well-maintained property is less risky, and lenders might offer better rates.

In addition to these traditional requirements, lenders also consider the borrower's experience in real estate. Investors with a proven track record of successful projects may find themselves with more negotiation power.

Presenting a detailed business plan or investment strategy that demonstrates how the loan will be used to enhance profitability can also influence a lender's willingness to provide more favorable terms.

Increasing Cash Flow and Managing Debt: Key to Long-Term Success

Effective real estate investing is not just about securing financing; it's also about maintaining healthy cash flow and managing debt strategically. Increasing cash flow involves optimizing rental income, minimizing vacancies, and implementing cost-effective property management practices. Some strategies include raising rental rates in line with market trends, reducing operating expenses, and enhancing property amenities to attract higher-paying tenants.

Managing debt is equally important. A comprehensive debt management plan helps you stay on top of multiple loan payments, reduce high-interest debt, and utilize effective refinancing strategies. Regularly monitoring your debt-to-income ratio and maintaining a strong credit profile are essential steps to ensure continued access to favorable financing terms and pave the way for future investments.

Expanded Cash Flow Strategies

In addition to basic cost-saving methods, investors can explore creative ways to increase cash flow:

- **Short-Term Rentals:** Consider converting properties into short-term rental units through platforms like Airbnb, which can significantly boost income in the right markets.

- **Energy Efficiency Upgrades:** By improving energy efficiency (e.g., adding solar panels or upgrading insulation), you can lower utility costs and potentially charge higher rents, appealing to eco-conscious tenants.

Another powerful strategy is to reinvest part of the profits back into the property by upgrading kitchens, bathrooms, or common areas. These value-added renovations can justify significant rent increases and attract a higher caliber of tenants, resulting in better cash flow over time.

Additionally, negotiating long-term lease agreements with tenants may help create stability and predictability in your cash flow projections.

Creative Financing Options: Thinking Outside the Box

Investors can also explore creative financing options that provide alternatives to traditional loans:

- **Seller Financing:** In this arrangement, the seller directly finances the purchase, usually in the form of a loan. Seller financing can be a beneficial option when conventional financing isn't available, as it often comes with flexible terms.

- **Partnerships:** Partnerships allow investors to pool resources, reduce individual risk, and share rewards. This is particularly useful when tackling large or complex investment projects.

Joint ventures and syndications are additional partnership models that can enable you to access capital and share expertise. In these cases, an investor may join forces with other partners who have different skill sets—one may focus on financing while another handles property management.

Creative financing doesn't stop with partnerships; using options like lease-to-own agreements can offer potential tenants the opportunity to purchase the property at a later date, creating an additional revenue stream for the investor.

Additionally, exploring crowdfunding platforms can open new avenues for securing financing. These platforms allow multiple investors to contribute smaller amounts toward a larger project, providing access to capital that may not be available through traditional lending. This method not only spreads risk but also taps into a network of investors who may bring valuable expertise and connections to the table.

Risk Management in Real Estate Financing

Managing risk is a fundamental aspect of successful real estate investing. Effective risk management ensures that investors can mitigate potential losses and maintain profitability even when unexpected challenges arise. Here are key strategies for managing risk in real estate financing:

- **Diversification:** Spreading investments across different property types and geographic locations can reduce exposure to market volatility in any single area.

- **Insurance:** Obtaining comprehensive insurance coverage, including property, liability, and title insurance, protects against unforeseen events such as natural disasters, accidents, or legal disputes.

- **Contingency Funds:** Setting aside a portion of your budget for unexpected expenses ensures that you can address repairs or vacancies without jeopardizing your financial stability.

- **Thorough Due Diligence:** Conducting detailed inspections and financial analyses before purchasing a property helps identify potential issues that could affect the investment's profitability.

Implementing these risk management strategies can help safeguard your investments and provide a buffer against financial uncertainties.

Tax Considerations for Real Estate Investors

Understanding the tax implications of real estate investing can significantly impact your net returns. Here are some key tax considerations to keep in mind:

- **Depreciation:** Real estate investors can deduct depreciation on their properties, which helps reduce taxable income without affecting cash flow.

- **1031 Exchanges:** This provision allows investors to defer capital gains taxes by reinvesting proceeds from the sale of one property into another similar property.

- **Mortgage Interest Deduction:** Interest paid on mortgages is deductible, which can lower your overall tax liability.

- **Capital Gains Taxes:** Long-term investments held for more than a year are subject to lower capital gains tax rates compared to short-term investments.

- **Operating Expenses:** Expenses such as property management fees, maintenance costs, and utilities are deductible and can help reduce taxable income.

Consulting with a tax professional can help you navigate these considerations and optimize your investment strategy for tax efficiency.

Legal Aspects of Financing Real Estate

Navigating the legal landscape is crucial for real estate investors to ensure compliance and protect their investments. Key legal aspects include:

- **Contracts and Agreements:** Clearly written contracts for purchases, leases, and financing agreements help prevent disputes and misunderstandings.

- **Zoning Laws and Regulations:** Understanding local zoning laws ensures that your investment aligns with permissible property uses and development plans.

- **Title Searches and Insurance:** Conducting thorough title searches prevents ownership disputes, and title insurance protects against potential title defects.

- **Fair Housing Laws:** Compliance with fair housing regulations ensures that your rental practices are non-discriminatory and legally sound.

- **Entity Formation:** Structuring your investments through legal entities like LLCs can provide liability protection and potential tax benefits.

Working with a real estate attorney can help you address these legal aspects effectively, ensuring that your investments are secure and compliant with all relevant laws.

Exit Strategies for Real Estate Investments

Having a clear exit strategy is essential for maximizing returns and minimizing risks when exiting a real estate investment. Common exit strategies include:

- **Selling the Property:** Selling allows investors to realize their profits and reinvest in new opportunities. Timing the sale to coincide with market highs can enhance returns.

- **Refinancing:** Refinancing can provide liquidity by tapping into the property's equity, allowing investors to retain ownership while accessing funds for other investments.

- **Lease Option:** Offering a lease with an option to buy gives tenants the opportunity to purchase the property in the future, providing a steady income stream and potential sale.

- **1031 Exchange:** As mentioned earlier, a 1031 exchange allows investors to defer capital gains taxes by reinvesting in a similar property, facilitating continuous growth.

- **Holding the Property Long-Term:** Retaining ownership for an extended period can provide consistent rental income and benefit from property appreciation over time.

Selecting the right exit strategy depends on your investment goals, market conditions, and financial situation. Planning your exit strategy in advance ensures that you can act swiftly and decisively when the time comes to liquidate your investment.

Case Studies: Real-World Financing Successes and Challenges

Examining real-world examples can provide valuable insights into the practical application of financing strategies. Here are a few case studies illustrating different financing approaches:

1. Case Study 1: Leveraging a Conventional Loan for Long-Term Rental

- **Investor Profile:** Jane Doe, an experienced real estate investor with a strong credit history.

- **Financing Strategy:** Utilized a conventional loan with a 20%

down payment and favorable interest rates.

- **Outcome:** Successfully acquired a multi-family property, benefiting from stable rental income and property appreciation over 10 years.

2. Case Study 2: Utilizing Hard Money Loans for a Quick Flip

- **Investor Profile:** John Smith, new to real estate investing, aiming to flip properties.

- **Financing Strategy:** Secured a hard money loan to purchase and renovate a distressed property.

- **Outcome:** Completed the flip within 6 months, achieving a significant profit despite the higher interest rates associated with hard money loans.

3. Case Study 3: Creative Financing Through Partnerships

- **Investor Profile:** Sarah Lee, seeking to invest in commercial real estate.

- **Financing Strategy:** Formed a partnership with a financial investor, combining resources to purchase a commercial property.

- **Outcome:** Shared profits and responsibilities, successfully managing the property and achieving higher returns than solo investment.

PROPERTY WEALTH

These case studies demonstrate how different financing strategies can be tailored to fit various investment goals and circumstances. Learning from real-world experiences can help you make informed decisions and avoid common pitfalls in real estate financing.

Chapter 4
Due Diligence & Smart Acquisition

cquiring a property is a significant milestone in the journey of a real estate investor. Conducting thorough due diligence and making smart acquisition decisions are crucial for ensuring successful and profitable investments. In this chapter, we will explore the important aspects of conducting property inspections and evaluations, negotiating prices, structuring deals, and mitigating risks to avoid common pitfalls.

Conducting Property Inspections and Evaluations

The first step in the acquisition process involves conducting thorough property inspections and evaluations. This entails examining both the physical condition of the property and its financial performance. It is essential to engage qualified professionals, such as home inspectors, appraisers, and contractors, to assess the property's structural integrity, potential repairs or renovations required, and compliance with building codes.

Additionally, conducting a comprehensive financial analysis, including reviewing income and expense statements, tax records, and lease agreements, will provide insights into the property's current and future cash flow potential.

Expanding Property Evaluation to Include Environmental and Legal Considerations

While structural and financial assessments are crucial, investors should not overlook environmental and legal evaluations. This includes checking for potential environmental hazards like asbestos, lead paint, or underground storage tanks that could cause costly future liabilities.

Engaging environmental consultants and attorneys familiar with local regulations will help uncover these issues early, ensuring that you comply with environmental laws and avoid potential legal entanglements.

Verifying zoning regulations and land use rights are also key aspects, especially if you plan on modifying or developing the property.

Negotiating Prices and Structuring Deals

Negotiating prices and structuring deals is a critical skill that can greatly impact the profitability of an investment. Investors should thoroughly research the property's market value using comparable sales data and market trends.

Armed with this information, they can confidently negotiate the purchase price and terms with sellers. Structuring the deal involves considering factors such as financing contingencies, seller concessions, and any required repairs or improvements.

Striking the right balance between price, terms, and concessions is imperative to ensure a win-win situation for both the buyer and the seller.

Strengthening Negotiation with Creative Financing Solutions

To further enhance your deal-making capabilities, it is beneficial to explore creative financing solutions such as seller financing, lease-to-own options, or partnerships.

Seller financing, where the seller agrees to accept installment payments instead of a lump sum, can provide flexibility and reduce upfront capital outlay. Lease-to-own options allow investors to test a property's cash flow potential before committing fully.

Additionally, entering into joint ventures or partnerships with other investors can allow for the pooling of resources and risk-sharing, providing access to deals that might otherwise be unattainable.

Mitigating Risks and Avoiding Common Pitfalls

Mitigating risks is an essential component of smart acquisition. Investors must identify and assess potential risks associated with a property or the transaction itself.

Common risks include environmental concerns, zoning restrictions, title issues, and unforeseen expenses.

Engaging professionals, such as real estate attorneys and title agencies, can provide valuable assistance in uncovering and addressing these risks.

Utilizing contingency clauses in the purchase agreement, such as inspection and financing contingencies, allows investors to back out of the deal if the identified risks are unacceptable or unmanageable.

Expanding Risk Mitigation with Insurance and Market Shifts

Beyond the immediate risks of the property, investors should also consider long-term risks like market volatility and economic downturns. Acquiring property insurance, including liability coverage and disaster-specific policies, is an essential safeguard against unforeseen losses.

Additionally, being aware of local and global economic trends, such as interest rate fluctuations, changing tax laws, and emerging neighborhood dynamics, will help investors anticipate market shifts and prepare contingency plans. For instance, diversifying your property portfolio or opting for properties in recession-resistant sectors, like affordable housing, can help mitigate long-term risks.

Avoiding Common Pitfalls

Avoiding common pitfalls is paramount in the acquisition process. One common pitfall is overestimating rental income or underestimating expenses, leading to negative cash flow. To avoid this, investors should conduct thorough market research to accurately project rental rates and expenses.

Another pitfall is failing to account for potential vacancies. Investors should have contingency plans in place to manage vacancies and minimize their impact on cash flow.

Additionally, overlooking crucial factors such as location, neighborhood dynamics, and local regulations can result in unintended consequences. Diligence and attention to detail are vital in identifying and navigating potential pitfalls.

Enhancing Due Diligence with Technology and Data Analytics

One of the most powerful tools in today's real estate landscape is technology. Using advanced data analytics tools can help investors assess rental markets, evaluate property values, and even predict future trends based on historical data.

Platforms like CoStar, Zillow's economic insights, or software that tracks cap rates and rental income can add a new level of precision to your property evaluations. Moreover, using tools like drones or 3D property scans can provide detailed property inspections, offering a thorough understanding of a property's condition remotely.

One final consideration in the acquisition process is understanding the community and neighborhood where the property is located. While property inspections and financial analysis are critical, they don't provide the full picture of the property's long-term potential. Understanding the social dynamics, future development plans, and local economy of the area can be just as important.

For example, an investor purchasing a multi-family property in an up-and-coming neighborhood might benefit from rising property values and increased rental demand in the future. Conversely, buying in a declining neighborhood, no matter how well-maintained the property is, can limit future returns.

Engaging with local real estate agents, attending community meetings, and researching local government initiatives can provide insight into the future prospects of the neighborhood. In particular, upcoming infrastructure projects like new transportation hubs, schools, or commercial developments can signal future appreciation in property values.

On the flip side, signs of population decline, high crime rates, or businesses leaving the area can serve as red flags that the property may not yield the expected return on investment. Understanding these macro trends, combined with the micro details of the property itself, helps investors make well-rounded acquisition decisions.

Another crucial factor is understanding the competition within the local market. Real estate investors should evaluate not only current market conditions but also the inventory and pricing of similar properties in the area. Are there a lot of similar properties for sale or rent? Are other investors targeting the same market segment, such as vacation rentals or student housing?

Conducting a competitive analysis helps determine whether your property stands out and whether you can adjust your acquisition strategy to better fit market demand. For example, if you're investing in a rental property and the market is saturated, offering value-added features like updated amenities or flexible lease terms can make your property more attractive.

Additionally, it's important to think about the long-term maintenance and operational costs of the property. While the upfront price and financing are critical, the ongoing expenses for repairs, property management, and upgrades should not be overlooked.

Budgeting for capital expenditures (CapEx) such as roof repairs, HVAC system replacements, and landscaping will help protect your cash flow and profitability. Investors should have a clear understanding of when major repairs will be necessary and ensure these costs are factored into their financial analysis before closing the deal.

Finally, don't underestimate the value of tenant quality when evaluating rental properties. Property in perfect condition with excellent financials can still turn into a headache if the tenant base is unreliable or high turnover leads to costly vacancies. Screen potential tenants carefully by reviewing their credit history, employment status, and rental history. Keeping tenant turnover low and ensuring stable rental income can make the difference between a good investment and a great one.

Conducting thorough due diligence and making smart acquisition decisions are essential for successful real estate investments. This involves conducting thorough property inspections and evaluations, skillfully negotiating prices and structuring deals, and mitigating risks to avoid common pitfalls. By meticulously assessing properties, engaging in effective negotiations, and identifying and mitigating risks, investors position themselves for profitable and sustainable investments.

Chapter 5
Mastering Cash Flow – The Art of Efficient Property Management

When it comes to real estate investing, cash flow is king. It is the driving force behind profitability and long-term success.

In this chapter, we will delve into advanced property management techniques, discuss how to find reliable tenants, set competitive rental rates, reduce vacancy rates, and employ strategies to boost rental income. These strategies are vital in sustaining high returns on your investments.

Efficient Property Management Techniques and Systems

Efficient property management is the foundation of successful rental properties. It's not just about collecting rent—it's about creating a streamlined operation that maximizes profits and minimizes stress.

1. **Automated Systems for Property Management:** Modern property management systems help automate many manual processes, such as rent collection, tenant communication, and maintenance requests. Using property management software not only reduces human error but also saves time and resources, allowing you to focus on strategic growth. By setting up automatic rent reminders and payments, property owners can

reduce late payments and streamline cash flow.

2. **Routine Maintenance and Repairs:** Establish a detailed maintenance and repair schedule to prevent small issues from becoming costly emergencies. Proactive maintenance not only ensures that properties stay in good condition but also improves tenant satisfaction and retention. Preventative measures, such as regular HVAC inspections or roof checks, are significantly more cost-effective than emergency repairs.

3. **Financial Organization and Record Keeping:** Having organized financial records is crucial for keeping track of income, expenses, and profitability. A well-organized system helps you keep an eye on cash flow while ensuring you're prepared for tax time. Use accounting software to track every transaction, including repair costs, utilities, and tenant deposits, to ensure you're maximizing your return on investment (ROI).

4. **Staying Compliant with Legal Requirements:** Keeping up with local, state, and federal regulations can protect you from costly fines and legal issues. Laws governing tenant rights, rent control, eviction procedures, and safety regulations frequently change. Hiring a legal advisor or using compliance management software will ensure you stay within legal bounds and avoid potential litigation.

Finding Reliable Tenants

Securing reliable tenants is arguably the most critical component of maintaining a steady cash flow. Finding the right tenants reduces the risk of missed rent payments, damage to the property, and costly evictions. A robust tenant screening process can safeguard your investment.

1. **Screening Protocols:** Develop a detailed tenant screening protocol that includes credit and background checks, rental history, and income verification. By setting strict criteria, you ensure that prospective tenants are financially stable and have a solid rental history. Be sure to check for any history of late payments, evictions, or legal disputes, as these are red flags.

2. **Interviewing Tenants:** In addition to standard screening procedures, take the time to interview prospective tenants. Look for clear communication, professionalism, and responsibility. Ask why they are moving, how long they intend to stay, and what they value most in a rental property. This adds a personal touch and can help you gauge whether the tenant will be a good fit.

3. **Using Rental Verification Forms:** As part of your screening process, use rental verification forms to request detailed information from previous landlords. This helps confirm whether the tenant has a history of timely payments and good behavior. Accompany this with a signed Release of Information Authorization Form to protect yourself legally and ensure transparency.

Enhancing Tenant Satisfaction and Retention

A crucial part of reducing vacancy rates and maintaining a healthy cash flow is tenant satisfaction. Happy tenants are more likely to renew their leases, take better care of the property, and recommend it to others. Building trust through consistent and open communication can significantly impact tenant retention. Here are a few practical ways to ensure tenant satisfaction:

Proactive Communication

Keep tenants informed about important updates, such as maintenance schedules or any potential disruptions. Use digital communication tools to create a seamless flow of updates. Sending out regular newsletters or using tenant portals can help maintain strong landlord-tenant relationships.

Response Time to Maintenance Requests

One of the most significant frustrations tenants have is slow maintenance response. Implement a system that prioritizes urgent repairs and clearly communicates timelines for non-urgent requests. Fast responses to maintenance requests not only keep tenants happy but also prevent minor issues from becoming costly repairs.

Tenant Amenities and Community Building

Tenants are increasingly looking for properties that offer more than just a place to live. Consider providing shared amenities such as high-speed internet, gym facilities, or communal spaces for residents. Hosting occasional community events, like holiday parties or BBQs, can help foster a sense of community, making tenants feel more at home and less inclined to leave.

Setting Competitive Rental Rates

Setting the right rental rate is an art, requiring a balance between maximizing revenue and remaining competitive in the market. Here are the steps to finding that sweet spot:

1. **Market Research & Comparable:** Conduct thorough market research on the rental rates in your area. Look at properties similar to yours in terms of size, location, and amenities. Websites like Zillow or Rentometer can provide valuable data on comparable rents, helping you assess where your property stands.

2. **Understanding Demand Drivers:** Location, proximity to schools, access to public transportation, and neighborhood safety are all factors that influence rental pricing. Understanding what drives demand in your local market is key to setting rates that attract quality tenants while maximizing your earnings.

3. **Flexible Pricing Models:** Consider offering flexible pricing models, such as offering discounts for long-term leases or slightly adjusting rent for tenants who pay multiple months upfront. Offering perks like free utilities or parking in exchange for a higher rental rate can also work as a competitive advantage.

Reducing Vacancy Rates

Vacant properties are a cash flow killer. Reducing vacancy rates ensures a consistent revenue stream and saves on costs associated with tenant turnover, such as cleaning, repairs, and marketing. Here's how to keep your properties occupied:

1. **Effective Marketing:** In the digital age, how you market your property matters. Utilize high-quality photos, create engaging online listings, and highlight unique selling points like modern amenities, pet-friendly policies, or proximity to entertainment. Utilize platforms like Zillow, Craigslist, and social media to reach a broad audience.

2. **Prompt Responses and Showings:** When prospective tenants inquire about a property, responding quickly can make all the difference. Offer flexible showing times and ensure your listings have professional photos and clear details to generate interest. Consider virtual tours to reach a larger audience.

3. **Tenant Retention Strategies:** Retaining tenants is as important as finding new ones. Offering lease renewal incentives such as minor upgrades, rental discounts, or gift cards can encourage tenants to stay. Building a positive landlord-tenant relationship through clear communication and prompt responses to concerns also leads to lower turnover.

Increasing Rental Income

Once your property is occupied, the next step is finding ways to increase rental income. Small upgrades, periodic rent reviews, and additional services can help you boost profits without significantly increasing operating costs.

1. **Property Upgrades:** Renovating key areas of the property, like the kitchen or bathroom, can justify higher rental rates. Consider adding modern appliances, updating flooring, or enhancing curb

appeal. Properties with energy-efficient systems or smart home technology may also command higher rents.

2. **Additional Revenue Streams:** Think beyond rent. Offering optional services, such as pet fees, parking spaces, laundry facilities, or storage units, can add to your income. Explore opportunities to charge for amenities that tenants value.

3. **Rent Increases:** As market conditions change, you should review your rental rates annually. Implement small, consistent increases to keep pace with inflation and rising costs, ensuring your investment remains profitable. Ensure your lease agreements include clauses for periodic rent increases to maintain flexibility.

Building a Reputable Landlord Brand

In competitive rental markets, building a reputation as a reliable and considerate landlord can help set you apart from the competition. Word-of-mouth recommendations, positive online reviews, and a strong landlord brand can help attract and retain tenants.

Online Reviews: Encourage satisfied tenants to leave positive reviews on rental platforms or Google. Positive testimonials go a long way in reassuring prospective tenants that your property is well-managed and the landlord is responsive.

Reputation Management: Actively managing your reputation by responding to reviews, both positive and negative, shows that you value tenant feedback and are committed to improving your services.

Conclusion

Maximizing cash flow in real estate investments is a multifaceted process that requires careful attention to property management, tenant satisfaction, and market dynamics. By implementing efficient property management techniques, finding reliable tenants, setting competitive rental rates, and employing strategies to reduce vacancies, you create a foundation for consistent profitability.

Furthermore, leveraging modern technology and staying ahead of market trends can give you an edge in attracting and retaining quality tenants. Real estate investment success is not solely determined by acquiring properties but by actively managing and optimizing them to ensure long-term financial growth.

As you continue on your investment journey, the key is to remain flexible, adaptive, and committed to both the financial and human aspects of property management.

The rewards of maximizing cash flow are not only immediate but contribute to the long-term value of your real estate portfolio. In the next chapter, we will explore how proactive capital expenditures and regular property maintenance can protect and grow your real estate investment for years to come.

Chapter 6
Scaling Your Empire – Expanding and Safeguarding Your Real Estate Portfolio

---•●•---

As you venture deeper into real estate investing, it's natural to start thinking about how to grow your portfolio. Whether you're aiming for financial freedom, generational wealth, or simply a more diverse income stream, scaling your investments is a thrilling milestone. However, it's not without its challenges. This chapter will walk you through some tried-and-true strategies for expanding your portfolio, saving on taxes, and diversifying to minimize risk. It's not just about growing bigger—it's about growing smarter.

Scaling and Expanding Your Portfolio

At its core, scaling a real estate portfolio means growing it in a way that's sustainable and strategic. You don't just want to add properties for the sake of numbers; you want to make sure that every new investment brings value and aligns with your long-term goals. This starts with having a clear plan. Ask yourself: What kind of properties do I want to focus on? Am I willing to venture into new markets or stay within my comfort zone? What's my risk tolerance?

- **Knowing When to Pull the Trigger**: Timing is everything in real estate. You don't want to expand too quickly, leaving yourself cash-strapped. On the other hand, waiting for the "perfect moment" can cause you to miss out on valuable opportunities. The key is to stay informed. Dive deep into local market trends, follow interest rate shifts, and keep an eye on economic factors like job growth and population influxes. The more data you have, the easier it becomes to make smart decisions.

- **The Power of Equity**: One of the beautiful things about real estate is that you can leverage what you already own to grow your portfolio. If your properties have appreciated over time, you can use that built-up equity to fund future investments. A cash-out refinance or a home equity line of credit (HELOC) can provide you with the capital to buy your next property without draining your savings. Just make sure that the returns on your new investment justify taking on the additional debt. Leveraging can be a powerful tool—if used wisely.

And don't overlook partnerships. Maybe you've reached a point where doing it all on your own feels overwhelming. Teaming up with a fellow investor, developer, or even a property management company can help you scale faster. Collaboration isn't just about sharing resources; it's also about pooling knowledge and expertise. Sometimes, having another set of eyes on a deal can make all the difference.

Utilizing 1031 Exchanges and Other Tax-Saving Strategies

Ah, taxes—the necessary evil that eats into your hard-earned profits. But as a savvy investor, you don't have to settle for paying a huge chunk of your gains to the government. Enter the 1031 exchange. It's one of the most effective ways to defer capital gains taxes, allowing you to reinvest your profits into another property and grow your portfolio more quickly.

- **Making the Most of 1031 Exchanges**: At first glance, a 1031 exchange might seem complex, with its tight timelines and legal requirements. But once you get the hang of it, it can become a game-changer. Imagine this: You sell a rental property you've owned for years, but instead of paying capital gains taxes, you use the money to purchase a larger, more lucrative property. Suddenly, you've got a new income stream, and Uncle Sam isn't taking a slice of your profits—yet. It's like playing chess, where each move sets you up for a bigger win down the road.

  However, it's not without its rules. You have 45 days to identify a "like-kind" property and 180 days to close the deal. It's a tight window, so having a solid plan in place is key. And don't forget to consult with professionals—having the right legal and financial guidance can help you avoid costly mistakes.

- **Beyond the 1031**: While the 1031 exchange gets all the glory, there are other tax-saving strategies you should have in your arsenal. Depreciation is a big one—by deducting the wear and tear on your properties, you can significantly lower your taxable income. And if you're willing to invest in energy-efficient upgrades like solar panels or better insulation, there are tax credits that can further reduce your tax bill. Think of these savings as more fuel for your growth—they free up capital that you can reinvest in future properties.

Diversifying Investments to Minimize Risk

Let's face it: no matter how smart you are, there's always an element of risk in real estate. The market fluctuates, economic conditions change, and unforeseen events—like a global pandemic—can throw even the best-laid plans off course. That's where diversification comes into play. By spreading your investments across different types of properties, markets, and even asset classes, you're protecting yourself from putting all your eggs in one basket.

- **Mixing It Up**: Residential real estate might be your bread and butter, but branching out into commercial or multi-family properties can give you added protection. For example, during an economic downturn, while residential rent might soften, commercial tenants—especially those with long-term leases— could provide a steady stream of income. It's all about balancing your risk.

And don't limit yourself geographically. If you've been solely focused on one city or region, consider expanding into new markets. Different areas can have vastly different economic conditions, so spreading your investments helps cushion the blow if one market starts to dip.

- **Beyond Real Estate**: It's not just about diversifying within real estate. As you grow your wealth, consider branching out into other investment vehicles like stocks, bonds, or even REITs (Real Estate Investment Trusts). Having a balanced portfolio that includes both real estate and more liquid assets can provide stability, especially during volatile times. The stock market, for example, tends to move inversely to real estate, meaning when one is down, the other might be up.

- **A Safety Net is Key**: No matter how diverse your portfolio is, make sure you have a rainy-day fund. Unexpected repairs, vacancies, or economic downturns can happen at any time. Having cash reserves set aside ensures that you're never caught off guard. After all, the best way to protect your investments is to be prepared for the worst—even while you hope for the best.

Final Words

Growing your real estate portfolio isn't just about collecting properties—it's about building a long-term, sustainable empire. By carefully scaling your investments, leveraging tax-saving strategies, and diversifying across multiple fronts, you can not only grow your wealth but also safeguard it. Real estate can be unpredictable, but with the right plan, knowledge, and safety nets in place, you'll be ready to navigate whatever comes your way.

SCOTT L GORDON

Chapter 7
Navigating Challenges and Building Skills

In the world of property management, challenges and mistakes are inevitable. Dealing with difficult tenants, resolving disputes, and handling maintenance and repair issues can seem daunting.

However, by adopting the right mindset and learning from past experiences, property managers can navigate these situations with poise and professionalism.

This chapter dives into strategies for overcoming difficulties, resolving disputes, and learning valuable lessons to prevent future pitfalls.

Understanding Tenants and Managing Behavior

Property managers often encounter tenants who are difficult to deal with for various reasons—whether due to late payments, disruptive behavior, or misunderstandings of lease agreements. Recognizing early signs of problematic tenant behavior can make all the difference, and understanding why tenants may act this way is key to handling these situations effectively.

Identifying Problematic Behaviors

Some tenants might "forget" rent due dates, while others might disregard property rules. Keeping detailed records of tenant behavior, like late payment logs or notices of complaints, is invaluable. These records not only help property managers maintain consistency, but they also serve as evidence if issues escalate.

Understanding the Root Causes

Sometimes, difficult behavior has less to do with disregard and more to do with personal struggles. By having conversations and showing empathy, property managers may discover that the tenant is going through financial hardship, a health issue, or other life events impacting their behavior. This approach builds rapport, which can make it easier to resolve conflicts in the future.

Effective Communication and Conflict Resolution

Communication is at the heart of successful property management. Having clear, open channels can prevent misunderstandings and foster stronger tenant relationships.

Building Effective Communication Channels

Setting up regular check-ins and establishing a preferred contact method are great first steps. Let tenants know that you're there to help and clarify how they should reach out for non-emergency issues versus emergencies.

Conflict Resolution Techniques

Active listening is a powerful tool in conflict resolution. When tenants know they're being heard, tensions often ease, allowing both sides to approach the issue more calmly. Effective conflict resolution can involve finding "win-win" solutions—such as negotiating flexible payment terms or offering temporary fixes until a larger issue can be addressed.

Maintaining Professional Boundaries

While being approachable is important, it's also necessary to maintain professional boundaries. If a tenant oversteps by making unreasonable demands or communicating at all hours, kindly remind them of your office hours or preferred communication methods. Consistency in enforcing these boundaries can prevent misunderstandings down the line.

Resolving Disputes: Mediation and Negotiation

Disputes between tenants and landlords are common, ranging from rent disagreements to disputes over property conditions. Effective dispute resolution requires a blend of mediation, negotiation, and sometimes legal support.

Using Mediation to Facilitate Solutions

In cases where the dispute has become too tense, involving a neutral third-party mediator can facilitate productive discussions. This mediator can help both parties reach an agreement that works for everyone. Mediation isn't about assigning blame; it's about finding a middle ground and preserving a respectful tenant-landlord relationship.

Negotiation Tactics

Negotiation skills are invaluable in property management. During negotiations, aim to remain calm, clear, and solution-oriented. For instance, if a tenant disputes repair costs, consider offering a temporary rent adjustment to ease the financial strain, as long as the tenant agrees to cover a portion of the repair costs later.

When Legal Action Becomes Necessary

Sometimes, despite best efforts, disputes escalate. When situations like unpaid rent or repeated lease violations persist, legal intervention may be necessary. Being familiar with local rental laws and keeping meticulous records can protect your position. If eviction or legal action is the final step, thorough documentation will ensure your actions are defensible.

Proactive Maintenance and Repair Solutions

Maintenance and repair issues are a given in property management. A proactive approach prevents minor issues from becoming major headaches, while also keeping tenants satisfied and properties well-maintained.

The Value of Routine Inspections

Prevention is often the best strategy. By scheduling regular inspections, property managers can identify and resolve small problems before they escalate. Simple actions, like regularly checking HVAC systems, plumbing, and electrical setups, ensure properties remain in top condition. Not only does this save time and money, but it also sends tenants a clear message that their comfort and safety are priorities.

Establishing an Emergency Response Plan

It's critical to have a clear, efficient plan for emergency repairs. Tenants should know who to contact in case of an urgent issue, whether it's a 24/7 hotline or an on-call maintenance team. Prompt responses to emergencies reduce the likelihood of costly damage and help maintain a positive tenant relationship.

Working with Reliable Contractors

Building a network of trusted contractors is essential. From plumbers to electricians, having reliable, licensed professionals on call means issues can be resolved quickly and effectively. Take time to thoroughly vet contractors, check references, and establish clear payment terms. Knowing who to call when problems arise makes the entire repair process smoother for both property managers and tenants.

Learning from Past Mistakes and Making Improvements

Mistakes are invaluable learning opportunities, especially in property management. Reflecting on past missteps, whether in tenant selection, lease drafting, or maintenance planning, can highlight areas for improvement.

Reflecting on Past Mistakes

Property managers must examine past errors to pinpoint what went wrong and why. Maybe it was a lenient screening process or an overlooked maintenance issue that led to a larger problem. By approaching mistakes with a growth mindset, property managers can uncover lessons that shape their future decisions.

Implementing Changes for Future Success

Recognizing past mistakes is only half the battle. Acting on those lessons is what drives improvement. Updating tenant screening policies, revising lease agreements, and tightening maintenance schedules are all positive steps that ensure mistakes aren't repeated. Continuous learning and adapting are key to long-term success in property management.

Finding a Reliable Property Manager

For investors, finding the right property manager is critical to achieving a successful real estate investment. Here are some of the best places to start your search:

Referrals and Recommendations

Word of mouth is often the best way to find a quality property manager. Ask other real estate investors, landlords, or members of local real estate associations for recommendations. Personal referrals provide insights into the property manager's strengths, responsiveness, and management style.

Online Platforms and Real Estate Networks

Websites like Zillow, Rent.com, and Angie's List have directories where you can find property managers in your area. Social media platforms, particularly LinkedIn, are also useful for checking out potential property managers and their professional backgrounds.

Real Estate Associations and Networking Events

Local real estate or property management associations often have lists of reputable property management companies. Networking events, workshops, and seminars also offer opportunities to connect with experienced property managers and gain valuable insights.

Reading Reviews and Testimonials

Online reviews offer a snapshot of a property manager's reputation and track record. Check for consistent patterns in the feedback—whether it's praise for responsiveness or complaints about slow repairs—to gauge how they're likely to handle your property.

Qualities of a Good Property Manager

Finding the right property manager goes beyond availability; it's about identifying someone who's equipped with the skills and knowledge to effectively manage rental properties.

Strong Communication Skills

Clear and effective communication is essential for handling tenant inquiries, coordinating with contractors, and keeping property owners informed. A good property manager will listen to tenant concerns and promptly address them to maintain positive relationships.

Exceptional Organizational Skills

From handling maintenance schedules to managing financial records, property managers juggle numerous responsibilities. Staying organized ensures that nothing falls through the cracks, helping maintain smooth property operations.

Knowledge of Real Estate Laws

Understanding landlord-tenant laws, fair housing regulations, and other legal requirements is a must. A knowledgeable property manager can navigate legal matters, ensuring properties comply with local and federal regulations.

Problem-Solving Skills and Financial Acumen

A property manager should be able to resolve conflicts and address maintenance issues quickly. They should also have a solid grasp of budgeting, accounting, and financial reporting to handle rent collection and manage expenses effectively.

Final Words

Overcoming challenges, resolving disputes, and learning from mistakes are critical skills in property management. By establishing open communication, implementing conflict resolution strategies, adopting proactive maintenance, and reflecting on past experiences, property managers can build a foundation for successful, long-term property management. For investors, partnering with a reliable and competent property manager ensures a smoother, more profitable journey in real estate.

Chapter 8
Smart Exits—Timing, Tax Strategies, and Planning for the Future

· ● ·

Making the decision to sell a real estate investment is about more than just cashing out; it's about understanding market timing, leveraging tax benefits, and planning for future financial security.

A well-timed exit can significantly boost your overall return, while careful planning can minimize taxes and help position your assets for long-term growth.

This chapter will guide you through the steps for exiting investments profitably and strategically, covering everything from identifying the right time to sell to exploring tax-deferment strategies and building a roadmap for retirement. By the end, you'll have a toolkit for making decisions that align with both your immediate goals and your financial future.

Selling Properties at the Right Time for Maximum Profit

Understanding Market Cycles

Real estate markets move in cycles, influenced by factors like economic growth, interest rates, and local demand. Recognizing where we are in this cycle is crucial. Generally, markets move through four stages: recovery, expansion, hyper-supply, and recession. In the expansion phase, prices and rents rise due to high demand, making it an ideal time for many investors to sell. In contrast, during hyper-supply, the influx of properties can drive prices down. By analyzing local and national economic indicators, such as employment rates, new construction trends, and occupancy levels, investors can better understand when it's time to sell.

Assessing Property Performance

Evaluating whether a property has reached its maximum potential requires a close look at various performance metrics. Net operating income (NOI), cash-on-cash return, and occupancy rates are indicators of a property's profitability. For instance, if a property is showing signs of slowed rental growth or increased vacancy, it might be worth considering a sale.

Additionally, assessing the local rental market for competitiveness helps determine whether retaining the property is beneficial or if an exit could yield a higher return on investment.

Effective Marketing and Presentation

A property's perceived value is significantly influenced by its presentation. Before listing, consider cost-effective renovations, like updating the landscaping, refreshing paint, or modernizing appliances to make the property more appealing to potential buyers.

Marketing strategies should leverage digital platforms—professional photos, virtual tours, and engaging descriptions on listing websites attract more attention and drive higher offers. Collaborating with an experienced real estate agent with a deep knowledge of the market can also enhance exposure, attract serious buyers, and help achieve the best price.

1031 Exchanges and Tax Implications

Understanding 1031 Exchanges

A 1031 exchange is a powerful tool for investors seeking to defer capital gains taxes. By reinvesting in another "like-kind" property, you can grow your portfolio without the tax hit from a sale. However, these exchanges come with specific rules: for example, you must identify a replacement property within 45 days and close within 180 days. Exploring similar properties in high-growth areas or diversifying asset types can maximize your returns while deferring taxes.

Tax Implications of Property Sales

Selling a property has tax consequences, including capital gains taxes and potential depreciation recapture. Capital gains taxes apply to the profit from the sale, while depreciation recapture taxes are owed on any deductions claimed for property depreciation. Fortunately, investors can minimize these through planning.

Consider techniques like installment sales or opportunity zone investments, which may reduce immediate tax liabilities. Additionally, working with a tax professional can help identify applicable deductions and ensure you're prepared for any tax obligations well in advance of your sale.

Crafting Exit Strategies and Planning for Retirement

Importance of a Defined Exit Strategy

A defined exit strategy ensures that your goals, market timing, and personal finances are aligned. Investors can choose from various exit approaches, such as selling to individual buyers, working with REITs, or gradually releasing equity through property trusts.

Evaluating market conditions, setting realistic goals, and pinpointing potential buyers allows you to anticipate possible sale scenarios and capitalize on favorable market conditions.

Integrating Real Estate into Retirement Planning

Real estate can play a key role in creating a retirement plan that combines passive income, diversification, and financial security. Strategies for incorporating real estate into retirement include diversifying assets, projecting rental income for future expenses, and gradually transitioning active properties to passive ones (like REITs or real estate funds).

The goal is to balance immediate profits with sustainable income for your retirement years. Real estate offers a unique advantage here: its potential for appreciation and cash flow can provide long-term security, helping cover retirement expenses and providing a legacy for future generations.

Conclusion

A thoughtful approach to exiting real estate investments can set you up for future financial success. By timing your sale with market cycles, assessing property performance, maximizing tax advantages, and planning with retirement in mind, you position yourself to make informed, impactful decisions.

Remember to rely on trusted professionals—real estate agents, financial advisers, and tax consultants—to guide you in navigating complex tax codes and market dynamics. In doing so, you'll maximize your returns, strengthen your financial foundation, and enjoy a smooth transition from one phase of your investment journey to the next.

SCOTT L GORDON

Chapter 9
Investing in the Digital Age— Harnessing Technology for Real Estate Success

The digital revolution is reshaping every facet of real estate investing. From the way properties are found and financed to property management and emerging rental trends, technology offers a wide range of tools to help investors streamline and scale their portfolios like never before.

This chapter explores how to harness the power of technology and online platforms to make finding, financing, and managing properties more efficient and profitable. We'll also examine the impact of emerging trends such as short-term rentals and co-living spaces, which are transforming real estate into an increasingly dynamic and tech-driven industry.

Utilizing Technology and Online Platforms for Property Investment

Finding Properties

Online platforms have revolutionized how investors discover properties. From residential listings to commercial real estate, technology gives investors the ability to browse and evaluate a vast array of properties across multiple markets with ease.

Websites like Zillow, Realtor.com, and LoopNet, along with specialized real estate databases, allow investors to access property details, market insights, and investment analysis tools all in one place.

Data analytics has also become a game-changer, enabling investors to evaluate neighborhood trends, rental rates, and long-term property values. By leveraging these resources, investors can make faster, data-driven decisions that align with their portfolio goals.

Property Financing

Securing funding is often one of the biggest hurdles in real estate investing, but digital financing platforms have opened up new possibilities. Online mortgage services, crowdfunding platforms, and peer-to-peer lending provide alternative ways to secure financing quickly.

For example, platforms like Fundrise and PeerStreet allow investors to participate in real estate projects through fractional investments, lowering the capital barrier and making it easier to diversify.

Online mortgage comparison tools and automated loan pre-qualification streamline the process, allowing investors to explore financing options and secure capital efficiently.

Digital Due Diligence

Performing due diligence is a critical step in the investment process, and digital tools make it easier to vet properties thoroughly.

Virtual tours, property history reports, and digital document management systems enable investors to assess property conditions, market value, and compliance history from their devices. With tools like Google Earth, investors can even evaluate the surrounding area and local amenities.

Additionally, platforms that provide neighborhood statistics and crime rates give a fuller picture of the property's environment. Conducting thorough research online can reduce the need for costly on-site visits and ensure that each investment is a sound one.

Incorporating Automation for Property Management

Streamlining Tenant Management

Automation in property management can drastically cut down the time and effort required to handle tenants and maintenance. Property management software, such as Buildium, AppFolio, and Cozy, offers features like automated rent collection, digital lease signing, and tenant screening. Automated reminders and tenant portals simplify communication and payment collection, ensuring timely payments and easier record-keeping. This not only improves tenant satisfaction but also reduces the likelihood of late payments and disputes.

Maintenance and Repairs

Managing maintenance requests can be one of the more time-consuming aspects of property management. With automation, however, property owners can implement systems that allow tenants to submit requests online, prioritize urgent repairs, and even schedule routine maintenance tasks automatically.

Some software platforms are even equipped to connect property managers with local contractors and track the status of repairs. This level of automation ensures maintenance issues are addressed swiftly and that the property remains in top condition, enhancing its overall value and tenant retention.

Expense Tracking and Financial Reporting

Keeping track of expenses and preparing financial reports is essential for any real estate investor. Automated accounting tools in property management software simplify financial reporting, track income and expenses in real time, and even assist with tax preparation by organizing documents and generating tax-ready statements. This not only keeps investors informed about their cash flow and profitability but also enables faster, more accurate financial planning.

The Impact of Emerging Trends: Short-Term Rentals and Co-Living Spaces

Short-Term Rentals

Short-term rental platforms, like Airbnb and Vrbo, have redefined the rental landscape, offering a high-yield alternative to traditional leasing. Investors can maximize returns by renting properties to vacationers or business travelers on a short-term basis.

However, it's important to understand local regulations, as some cities restrict short-term rentals to protect long-term housing availability. By analyzing occupancy rates and adjusting nightly rates based on demand, investors can optimize income from short-term rentals, often exceeding what they might earn with a traditional tenant.

Co-Living Spaces

Co-living is a modern trend driven by younger demographics who seek affordable, community-focused living arrangements. Co-living properties typically offer shared amenities and communal spaces, creating a unique selling point in high-demand urban areas.

Investors interested in co-living spaces can appeal to millennials and Gen Z renters by offering amenities like Wi-Fi, communal workspaces, and flexible lease terms. This type of investment not only increases occupancy rates but also caters to a growing demand for flexible, social living environments, particularly in areas with a high cost of living.

With technology, investors can create highly customized strategies that cater to the demands of modern tenants. Think of how tech-savvy generations expect quick responses, digital accessibility, and convenience.

For real estate investors, this trend means that optimizing property listings, communication, and even tenant services are now part of attracting the best renters and maximizing returns. Embracing these new demands is part of staying competitive—and keeping properties in demand—within the digital age.

For investors open to innovation, the impact of these new real estate dynamics can be significant. Integrating smart home technology, offering flexible leasing options, and building an online presence are just a few strategies that tech-forward investors are using to stand out. These trends don't just make real estate management easier; they also help attract quality tenants who value the tech-enabled features that make their lives simpler.

Last Words

Investing in real estate has evolved with the rise of technology and new market trends. By embracing digital tools and staying ahead of trends like short-term rentals and co-living spaces, investors can enhance their strategies, increase efficiencies, and ultimately maximize their returns.

Incorporating automation not only saves time but also ensures that operations run smoothly, allowing investors to focus on growth and scaling their portfolios. In today's digital age, a tech-savvy approach is essential for any investor looking to stay competitive and profitable in the modern real estate market.

Chapter 10
Financial Freedom Through Real Estate

In today's rapidly changing financial landscape, achieving financial freedom has become a central goal for many individuals and families. The desire to break free from the constraints of traditional employment and gain control over one's financial future has never been more prevalent. Real estate, particularly rental property investments, offers a compelling pathway to build long-term wealth and create a sustainable stream of passive income.

As the cost of living continues to rise and economic uncertainties loom, the appeal of investing in real estate is growing. Unlike stocks or bonds, real estate offers tangible assets that can appreciate over time, providing a sense of security and stability. Moreover, the rental property market has shown resilience even in economic downturns, making it an attractive option for those seeking reliable income streams.

What sets real estate apart is its unique ability to generate passive income. Unlike a traditional job that requires constant effort and time, rental properties can provide income with minimal ongoing involvement. This allows investors to enjoy greater flexibility in their lives, whether that means pursuing personal passions, spending time with family, or even traveling.

Additionally, investing in rental properties opens doors to various financial benefits—from tax deductions and depreciation to appreciation and equity growth. These factors contribute to a comprehensive wealth-building strategy that can significantly enhance one's financial position over time.

However, embarking on this journey requires more than just capital; it necessitates a solid understanding of the real estate market, investment strategies, and effective property management techniques. With the right mindset and a commitment to continuous learning, anyone can navigate the complexities of real estate investing and achieve financial freedom.

Laying the Foundation for Financial Freedom
Setting Clear Goals and Crafting a Vision

Achieving financial freedom requires knowing exactly what you're aiming for. Whether you want to retire early, create a legacy, or simply enjoy more time and freedom, setting specific, measurable goals is crucial. Define your "why" and envision the lifestyle you want to lead, and from there, identify the milestones needed to reach it. This clarity in vision will help guide your investment decisions and keep you motivated during inevitable market fluctuations or property challenges.

Building a Portfolio with Purpose

It's not just about the number of properties you own—it's about building a portfolio that serves your unique financial goals.

For some, this may mean acquiring a handful of high-value properties, while for others, it could mean diversifying across various property types or locations. Having a clear plan for acquisition, management, and eventual sale of each property allows you to keep a balanced, income-generating portfolio.

Leveraging Mortgages for Property Investment

If you don't have the cash on hand to buy an investment property outright, obtaining a mortgage can be a powerful tool to make your real estate goals achievable. Financing a property with a mortgage lets you leverage your investment, allowing you to purchase a higher-value property than you might afford with cash alone. Here's how the process works and key factors to consider:

Understanding Mortgage Types and Terms

- **Fixed-Rate Mortgages:** With a fixed-rate mortgage, your interest rate stays the same throughout the loan term, providing predictable monthly payments. This can be advantageous for budgeting, especially if you plan to hold onto the property for many years.

- **Adjustable-Rate Mortgages (ARMs):** ARMs have an interest rate that may fluctuate based on market conditions. While they may offer lower initial rates, they come with a risk of higher future payments. ARMs can be beneficial if you're planning a shorter-term investment, such as a property you'll flip within a few years.

- **Interest-Only Loans:** Some investors opt for interest-only loans, which lower initial payments since you're only paying the interest portion of the loan. However, after the interest-only period, your payments may increase significantly, so you'll need a clear exit strategy, like refinancing or selling the property, before this happens.

Calculating Your Down Payment and Monthly Payments

- **Down Payment:** Many lenders require a down payment of 20-25% for investment properties. However, if you qualify for certain types of loans (like FHA or VA loans for qualifying investors), you may find options with lower down payments. Keep in mind that the higher your down payment, the lower your monthly mortgage payment and interest costs over time.

- **Monthly Payments and Cash Flow:** Ensuring the rent income covers your monthly mortgage payment, property taxes, insurance, and any maintenance costs is essential for generating positive cash flow. Calculate potential rental income and compare it to your projected monthly expenses, aiming for a buffer to manage unexpected costs.

Building Equity Over Time

One of the main benefits of using a mortgage is the ability to build equity as you pay down the loan. Each payment reduces your principal, increasing the property's equity. Over time, as property values rise, you could leverage this equity to refinance, access additional funds, or use it toward future investments.

Understanding Mortgage Interest and Tax Benefits

Mortgage interest on investment properties is generally tax-deductible, which can lower your taxable income and increase your overall return on investment (ROI).

Other deductible expenses include property management fees, repairs, and insurance premiums. It's wise to consult with a tax advisor to ensure you maximize these benefits and understand the tax implications fully.

Choosing the Right Loan and Lender

- **Interest Rates and Terms:** Shop around for lenders and compare interest rates, fees, and loan terms. Even a slight difference in interest rates can have a significant impact on your monthly cash flow and long-term profitability.

- **Pre-Approval:** Getting pre-approved not only helps you understand your budget but also strengthens your negotiating position. Sellers are often more inclined to accept offers from pre-approved buyers, giving you an edge in competitive markets.

- **Private and Hard Money Loans**: If traditional mortgage lenders don't meet your needs, consider alternative financing options, such as private lenders or hard money loans. While these options typically come with higher interest rates, they often have fewer restrictions, which can be beneficial in specific investment scenarios.

Risks and Challenges of Mortgage Financing

- **Market Risks:** A drop in property values could impact your investment's profitability, especially if you're heavily leveraged. Additionally, during periods of higher interest rates, refinancing options might become limited, affecting your cash flow.

- **Cash Flow Risks:** Even if you've done careful calculations, unexpected vacancies or maintenance issues can create cash flow shortfalls. It's crucial to have a reserve fund to handle these potential challenges.

- **Exit Strategy:** Always plan your exit strategy, whether that's holding, refinancing, or selling the property. Knowing when and how you'll move on from the mortgage can ensure you aren't caught off guard by shifting market conditions.

Using a mortgage to finance an investment property can be a strategic way to scale your portfolio without relying solely on cash.

By understanding the types of loans available, the impact on cash flow, and the tax benefits, you can make an informed decision that aligns with your investment strategy and risk tolerance.

Just remember that leveraging debt requires careful planning and risk management to ensure your investment remains profitable and sustainable.

Investment Strategies for Long-Term Success

Diversification to Reduce Risks

Investing in a mix of property types and geographic locations can protect against downturns in any single market.

Diversification also allows you to benefit from different income streams, such as residential rentals, commercial leases, and even short-term vacation rentals. This approach not only safeguards against risk but also enables you to capitalize on various growth opportunities.

Leveraging Partnerships for Greater Returns

Collaborating with other investors, whether through joint ventures or real estate investment groups, opens up new investment opportunities. Partnerships can provide additional capital, reduce financial risks, and enable you to tap into different areas of expertise, all while sharing profits and responsibilities. For many, the networking and shared knowledge that comes with partnerships are invaluable assets.

Preparing for Market Cycles and Changes

Understanding and anticipating market cycles is essential for any real estate investor. With knowledge of current trends, such as shifts in urbanization, emerging neighborhoods, or the growing demand for co-living spaces, you'll be well-positioned to make smarter investment choices and know when to buy, sell, or hold onto properties. Staying informed about market conditions, both local and national, will give you a competitive edge.

Planning for Early Retirement and Passive Income Streams

Creating a Passive Income Stream

Your portfolio of rental properties, when managed well, can generate income without requiring constant oversight. By structuring your portfolio for maximum cash flow and minimizing expenses, you can ensure that your properties provide a stable income stream throughout retirement. Additionally, setting up automated systems for property management or hiring a property manager can make this process even more seamless.

Estimating Retirement Needs and Timelines

Achieving financial freedom isn't a "one-size-fits-all" goal—it varies based on your lifestyle and retirement aspirations. Carefully assess your current expenses and anticipated lifestyle in retirement to calculate how much you'll need in passive income.

This will help you establish a timeline and determine the number and type of properties required to meet your financial needs. Setting achievable, incremental goals along the way will make your journey to retirement both motivating and sustainable.

Building a Sustainable Retirement Fund

Allocating a portion of your rental income toward a retirement fund provides a financial cushion that can protect against unforeseen market changes or property issues.

A carefully crafted retirement plan involves setting aside cash reserves, purchasing insurance, and occasionally reinvesting in your properties to increase their value over time. These strategies create a more secure and reliable income stream that can support you well into your later years.

Giving Back and Sharing Your Knowledge
The Importance of Mentorship

As you grow in your investment journey, you may find yourself in a position to help others. Sharing the lessons you've learned, the strategies that worked, and even the missteps along the way can be incredibly rewarding. Mentorship, teaching seminars, writing articles, or participating in community initiatives can create a positive impact on aspiring investors and even reinforce your own expertise.

Making a Positive Impact

Helping others achieve financial independence not only adds meaning to your success but also creates a supportive community around you.

By mentoring, you pass on valuable insights and inspire the next generation of investors, further strengthening the network of knowledgeable investors.

Engaging with the Community

Supporting local community initiatives or contributing to real estate education programs allows you to make a lasting impact. Whether through educational seminars, workshops, or donating to housing programs, giving back reinforces your values and fosters positive change.

Conclusion

Achieving financial freedom through real estate isn't merely about acquiring wealth—it's about building a life of security, choice, and influence. By setting clear goals, maintaining a flexible investment strategy, and continuously learning and adapting, you can create a portfolio that provides lasting wealth and independence.

Remember, real estate investing is a journey of growth and discovery. Whether you're just beginning or well on your way, stay focused on your "why," lean into your vision, and embrace the opportunities that arise. May your journey be filled with financial success, personal growth, and the fulfillment that comes from empowering others along the way.

Epilogue
Reflections and Words of Advice

—————————— • ● • ——————————

Looking back on this journey, I'm reminded of the countless steps it took to get here—the ups, the downs, and everything in between. Investing in rental properties has a way of teaching you something new every day.

You're not just dealing with numbers or assets; you're building a legacy, creating a sustainable way to support your future, and maybe even making a difference in the lives of others.

This book isn't just a guide; it's a collection of lessons I've learned on my path to financial freedom. I hope these pages have given you practical tools, useful insights, and, most of all, confidence.

Whether you're just getting started or already have a few properties under your belt, there's always something new to discover—and that's one of the most exciting parts of real estate.

Inspiring Others to Take Charge of Their Financial Future

One of the things I've learned along the way is how powerful it is to share what you know. Maybe you'll find yourself mentoring a friend, joining a community group, or even writing about your own experiences. By opening up about your successes, your failures, and everything you've learned, you're passing on a spark that just might ignite someone else's journey to financial independence.

Real estate isn't just about buildings or cash flow—it's about freedom, options, and the opportunity to live life on your terms. And that's a goal worth sharing.

A Real-World Look – What Makes a Good Investment?

To wrap up, let's get practical with a couple of examples. These two properties tell the story of what can make or break an investment.

A Winning Property: The Good

- **Location**: A well-kept, 3-bedroom, 2-bath home in a family-friendly neighborhood with good schools and low crime rates.

- **Purchase Price**: $200,000

- **Rental Income**: $1,800 per month

- **Monthly Expenses**: Around $300, covering property taxes, insurance, and maintenance.

- **Cash Flow**: $1,500 each month after expenses.

- **Appreciation Potential**: Values in this area have been rising, and the local economy is strong.

- **Resale Potential**: This location stays in demand, with high occupancy rates.

This property is a solid choice for its dependable cash flow, growth potential, and strong market demand. With these factors in place, it's likely to deliver income and value over the long term.

A Tricky Property – The Bad

- **Location**: A 1-bedroom, 1-bath condo in an area with limited amenities and higher crime rates.

- **Purchase Price**: $100,000

- **Rental Income**: $800 per month

- **Monthly Expenses**: $500, including HOA fees, maintenance, and insurance.

- **Cash Flow**: Only $300 a month after expenses.

- **Appreciation Potential**: Market values in this area have been dropping.

- **Resale Potential**: The property has high vacancy rates, making it difficult to rent or sell.

In this case, the limited income, high expenses, and low demand make it a much riskier investment. The cash flow is minimal, and the property lacks the growth potential that makes for a sound investment.

These examples show how important it is to evaluate each property on its own merits. Location, cash flow, and local demand all play a role in defining the success of an investment. Use these factors as your guide, and over time, you'll develop an eye for what works best.

In the end, real estate investing is more than just a way to build wealth—it's a path to independence, stability, and personal growth. As I look back, the most valuable lessons came not from the big wins but from the times when things didn't go as planned. Those moments taught me resilience, patience, and the importance of staying focused on the bigger picture.

To those who take up this journey, know that it's not a sprint but a marathon. You'll face setbacks, learn unexpected lessons, and gain insights that shape not just your portfolio but who you are. With every property, every tenant, and every challenge, you're building something far greater than income; you're creating a foundation for the life you've envisioned.

So, as you step forward, remember that you're not just investing in properties—you're investing in a future where your financial goals align with your personal values and ambitions. Here's to achieving financial freedom and, just as importantly, enjoying the journey along the way.

Take Action Today

As you close this book, I encourage you to take action. Whether it's attending a local real estate seminar, joining a property investment group, or simply setting your first investment goal, every small step counts.

The journey may be challenging, but it's also rewarding beyond measure. Investing in real estate is more than a financial decision— it's a commitment to a better future. So take that leap of faith. You've got this!

END

www.ingramcontent.com/pod-product-compliance
Lightning Source LLC
Chambersburg PA
CBHW040817120726
48005CB00012B/1440